DISNEY
Christmas
Cookbook

RECIPES

Joy Howard, with additional recipes by Cristina Garces
and Cynthia Littlefield

PHOTOGRAPHY

Joe St. Pierre

FOOD STYLING

Joy Howard

ILLUSTRATIONS

The Disney Storybook Art Team

DESIGN

Megan Youngquist

Published by Disney Press, an imprint of Buena Vista Books, Inc.
No part of this book may be reproduced or transmitted in any form or by any means,
electronic or mechanical, including photocopying, recording,
or by any information storage and retrieval system, without written permission from the publisher.
For information address Disney Press, 1200 Grand Central Avenue,
Glendale, California 91201.

Printed in the United States of America
First Hardcover Edition, October 2024
1 3 5 7 9 10 8 6 4 2

Library of Congress Control Number: 2023940838
FAC-067395-24200
ISBN 978-1-368-07497-1
Visit www.disneybooks.com

Disney
Christmas
Cookbook

DISNEP PRESS
Los Angeles • New York

Contents

Basics

The holidays bring a special kind of magic every year—and with an added dose of Disney, they're sure to be full of cheer! No matter how or where you celebrate, this cookbook is packed with dishes to keep you cozy, or to throw a feast with your family and friends. Aspiring chefs will find plenty of ways to keep bellies—not just stockings—happily stuffed, with food inspired by favorite Disney and Pixar characters.

Turn the page to discover fifty festive recipes—from breakfast, lunch, and dinner, to beverages, sides, snacks, and sweets. The recipes are rated on a five 🍪 scale, so if you're a beginner, don't worry! Start with an easier dish { 🍪 } and work your way up to the more complicated recipes { 🍪 🍪 🍪 🍪 🍪 }.

Now put on your apron and get ready to whip up some delicious treats that are so good, they'll make everyone's nice lists.

Before You Begin

Cooking is a lot of fun, but before you get started, there are some important things to remember. Always, always ask a parent for permission. If you need to use a stove, an oven, a blender, or a mixer for a recipe, make sure to ask an adult to help you. Even Santa needs help from the elves to get everything ready for Christmas. Here are a few other tips to keep in mind.

- If you have long hair, tie it back. You don't want it to end up in the food or near a hot stove.

- Make sure your clothing isn't loose enough to touch a stovetop burner. If you're wearing long sleeves, push them up to your elbows.

- Put on an apron to keep your outfit from getting stained.

- Wash your hands with water and soap for at least twenty seconds so they will be clean when you handle the ingredients.

- Take a few minutes to read the whole recipe so that nothing will come as a surprise once you get started.

- Gather all the equipment you'll need, such as measuring spoons, bowls, baking pans, and utensils, before you get out the ingredients.

Measuring Ingredients

To make sure a recipe turns out just the way it's supposed to, you need to measure ingredients exactly. Here are some helpful hints and tips.

- For liquids like milk, water, or oil, use a measuring cup with a spout designed for pouring.

- A dry ingredient, such as flour, sugar, or cocoa, should be spooned into a measuring cup without a spout. Then, to check that you have the exact amount, scrape the flat edge of a butter knife across the rim of the cup to remove any extra.

- A chunky ingredient should be spooned into a measuring cup and then patted gently, just enough to even out the top without packing it down. Shredded ingredients are also measured this way, unless the recipe specifies "packed."

- Brown sugar should be packed into a measuring cup to press out any air bubbles.

- Measuring butter is really easy if you use sticks that have tablespoon marks printed on the wrapper. All you have to do is slice the butter where the line is.

Safety First!

A good cook never forgets that safety always comes first in the kitchen. Here are some important rules to follow.

Using knives, peelers, graters, and small kitchen appliances

- Never use a kitchen appliance or sharp utensil without asking an adult for help.

- Always use a cutting board when slicing or chopping ingredients. Grip the knife handle firmly, holding it so that the sharp edge is facing downward. Then slice through the ingredient, moving the knife away from yourself.

- After slicing raw meat or fish, wash the knife (with an adult's help) as well as the cutting board. You should also wash your hands with water and soap for at least twenty seconds before working with other ingredients.

- If you drop a knife, don't try to catch it. Instead, quickly step back and let the knife fall to the countertop or floor before picking it up by the handle.

- When using a vegetable peeler, press the edge of the blade into the vegetable's skin and then push the peeler away from yourself. Keep in mind that the more pressure you use, the thicker the peeling will be.

- Use electrical appliances, such as mixers and blenders, in a cleared space far away from the sink and other wet areas. And always unplug a mixer or blender before scraping a mixture from the beaters or blades.

Working around hot things

- Always ask an adult for help around a hot stovetop or oven.

- Make sure to point the handle of a stovetop pan away from you so you won't knock into it and accidentally tip the pot over.

- Use pot holders every time you touch a stovetop pot or skillet—even if it's just the lid. You should also use pot holders whenever you put a pan in the oven or take it out.

- Remember, steam can burn! Be sure to step back a bit when straining hot foods, such as pasta or cooked vegetables.

- Don't forget to shut off the oven or stove burner when the food is done baking or cooking.

Preparing Fruits and Vegetables

It's important to wash produce before adding it to a recipe. Here are some tips for making sure fruits and vegetables are clean and ready to use.

- Rinse produce well under plain running water. Don't use soap! If the produce is firm, like an apple or carrot, rub the surface to help remove any garden soil or grit. You can put softer fruits and vegetables, such as berries and broccoli florets, in a small colander or strainer before rinsing.

- Use a vegetable brush to scrub vegetables that grow underground, like potatoes and carrots. You should also scrub any fruits and vegetables that grow right on the ground, such as cucumbers and melons.

- Dry washed produce with a paper towel or reusable cleaning cloth and cut off any bruised parts before using it in a recipe.

Cleaning Up

A good cook always leaves the kitchen as tidy as they found it. This means cleaning all the bowls, pots, pans, and utensils you used to prepare the recipe. Here are some tips for making sure everything is spick-and-span.

- Always ask an adult for help washing knives and appliances with sharp blades, such as a blender or food processor.

- As you cook, try to give each bowl and utensil a quick rinse as soon as you're done with it. That way leftover food or batter won't stick to it before you can wash it with soap and water.

- Put all the ingredients back where they belong so you'll know just where to find them the next time you cook.

- Wipe down your work area—including the countertop and sink—with a damp paper towel or reusable cleaning cloth.

- Double-check that all the appliances you used are turned off before you leave the kitchen.

- Hang up your apron, or put it in the laundry if it needs to be washed.

Breakfast

Rolly's Spotted Cranberry Pancakes	16
Monster-O's Spiced Breakfast Bars	18
Sleepy's Early-Riser Egg Biscuits	20
Belle's Classic Winter Porridge	22
Pooh Bear's Mini Honey Buns	24
Ariel's Puff Pastry Stars	26
Purr-fect French Toast	28
New York City Breakfast Pizzettes	30

Rolly's Spotted Cranberry Pancakes

These sweet pancakes, loaded with dried cranberries, walnuts, and chocolate chip "spots," are so filling they might just last you until Christmas dinner—and can even satisfy an appetite as big as Rolly's!

Directions

1. In a small bowl, whisk together the flour, sugar, baking powder, salt, and cinnamon.

2. In a medium bowl, mix together the milk, vanilla extract, butter, and egg. Whisk in the flour mixture until just wet, and carefully stir in the walnuts, cranberries, and chocolate chips.

3. Ask for an adult's help with the stove. Heat a large skillet over medium-low heat and grease with cooking spray. Spoon 2 tablespoons of batter into the skillet for each pancake, using the back of the spoon to spread the batter into a circular shape.

4. Cook each pancake until golden brown, about 1 minute per side.

Serves 4 to 6

Ingredients

1 cup all-purpose flour

2 Tbsp sugar

2 tsp baking powder

¼ tsp salt

½ tsp ground cinnamon

1 cup milk

2 tsp vanilla extract

2 Tbsp unsalted butter, melted

1 large egg

½ cup walnuts, chopped

½ cup dried cranberries

¾ cup mini or regular chocolate chips

Cooking spray

Tip

Try topping these pancakes with maple syrup or confectioners' sugar!

Ingredients

¼ cup dark brown sugar

¼ cup unsalted butter

½ cup honey

2 tsp vanilla extract

¼ tsp salt

¼ cup peanut or almond butter

2 cups whole-grain-oat cereal

¾ cup almonds, chopped

½ tsp cinnamon

Tip

It's easy to add any of your favorite ingredients to these bars, such as nuts; dried fruit like raisins, apricots, and coconut; or even chocolate chips! Have fun trying new combinations.

Monster-O's Spiced Breakfast Bars

Resembling Mike and Sulley's favorite "Monster-O's," these stocking stuffer–sized breakfast bars filled with whole-grain-oat cereal, honey, cinnamon, and nuts are the perfect treat to wake up to on Christmas morning.

Directions

1. Ask an adult for help with the oven. Preheat oven to 350°F. Grease an 8 x 8-inch baking pan, or line it with parchment paper.

2. Combine the dark brown sugar, butter, honey, vanilla extract, and salt in a medium saucepan over medium heat. Cook, stirring occasionally, until butter melts and the sugar completely dissolves. Stir in the peanut or almond butter.

3. Add the cereal, almonds, and cinnamon to the pot and stir to combine. Remove the pot from the heat, and pour the mixture onto the baking sheet, distributing it evenly along the bottom. Press down firmly.

4. Place the baking pan into the oven, and bake for 5 to 7 minutes. Let the mixture cool to room temperature before cutting into bars. These will keep for about a week at room temperature or a couple of weeks in the fridge or freezer.

Sleepy's Early-Riser Egg Biscuits

There's one time a year that Sleepy is an early riser—Christmas morning! These mini egg biscuits made with cheese and turkey bacon will bring everyone to the breakfast table.

Directions

1. Ask an adult for help with the oven. Preheat the oven to 350°F. Grease the cups of a standard-sized muffin tin. Separate the biscuit dough, and place each of the 10 biscuits into the muffin openings. (You'll have two empty cups left over.)

2. Bake the biscuit crusts for 5 minutes. While the biscuits are cooking, crack the eggs into a mixing bowl and add the milk, salt, and pepper. Whisk to combine, and stir in the broccoli and half of the cheddar cheese.

3. Remove the biscuits from the oven and use a wooden spoon to create a hole for the egg mixture.

4. Pour the egg mixture into each biscuit crust and top evenly with crumbled turkey bacon and the remaining cheddar cheese. Bake for 12 to 15 minutes more. Remove the biscuits from the oven and let cool for a few minutes before enjoying.

Makes 10

Ingredients

1 package of refrigerated biscuit dough

4 large eggs

2 tsp whole milk

¼ tsp salt

¼ tsp black pepper

¼ cup cooked broccoli florets, chopped

¼ cup shredded cheddar cheese, divided

6 strips cooked turkey bacon, crumbled

Tip

To make this dish vegetarian, just leave out the bacon—or use a vegetarian-friendly substitute!

Ingredients

4 cups milk

2 cups old-fashioned oats

1½ cups dried fruit mix
(like raisins, cranberries,
and apricots)

1½ tsp cinnamon

½ tsp ground ginger

¼ tsp ground nutmeg

¼ tsp ground cloves or
allspice

1½ tsp vanilla extract

¼ cup brown sugar

2 cups water

Chopped nuts, for
topping

Tip

*You can add a tablespoon
of your favorite jam or
even a splash of
Stitch's Hawaiian Eggnog
(page 104)
for different flavors!*

Belle's Classic Winter Porridge

On cold winter days, Belle likes to curl up by a cozy fire. The brown sugar and dried fruits in this spiced porridge are just as warming.

Directions

1. Ask for an adult's help with the stove. Warm the milk over medium heat in a large saucepan. Stir in the oats and cook for about 5 minutes, stirring constantly.

2. Stir in the fruit, spices, vanilla extract, brown sugar, and water. Turn the heat down to medium-low and simmer for 5 more minutes.

3. Portion out into 4 to 6 individual bowls. Top with chopped nuts.

Pooh Bear's Mini Honey Buns

Honey would make a perfect holiday gift for Winnie the Pooh! Inspired by Pooh Bear's favorite snack, these sticky sweet rolls are delicious enough to share.

Directions

1. Ask an adult for help with the oven. Preheat oven to 350°F. Combine the brown sugar and cinnamon in a small bowl and set aside.

2. Place the butter in another small bowl and carefully melt it in the microwave. Stir in the honey. Divide half of the mixture evenly among 8 to 10 cups of a standard-sized muffin tin.

3. Separate the biscuits and roll each one into a rope. Coil each rope into a circle, and pinch each end of the rope into the coil next to it so it is secure (or else they will unravel). Place each bun into a muffin tin cup, top with the remaining honey mixture, and sprinkle evenly with the brown sugar topping.

4. Bake for 12 to 15 minutes. Allow buns to cool completely before serving.

Makes 8 to 10

Ingredients

2 Tbsp brown sugar

1 tsp cinnamon

⅓ cup unsalted butter

⅓ cup honey

1 package refrigerated biscuit dough

Tip

For instructions on how to prepare the dough, turn to page 130.

Ingredients

1¼ cups fresh
strawberries, sliced

¼ cup, plus 1 tsp
granulated sugar, divided

4 oz cream cheese,
softened

½ tsp vanilla extract

2 large eggs

1 (17-oz) package puff
pastry, thawed

Flour, for dusting

Special Equipment

Jumbo
(3- to 4-inch)
star cookie cutter

Tip

*For instructions on how
to cut and fill these pastries,
turn to page 131.*

Ariel's Puff Pastry Stars

The sparkly stars that many families use to top their trees
resemble the starfishes Ariel loves spotting under the sea.
These star-shaped pastries, studded with sweet cream
cheese filling and berries, make a festive and surprisingly
simple breakfast during the holidays.

Directions

1. Ask an adult for help with the oven. Heat the oven to 400°F, and
    line two baking sheets with parchment paper. In a small bowl, stir
    together the strawberries and 1 teaspoon sugar. Set aside.

2. In another bowl, stir together the cream cheese, vanilla, 1 egg,
    and the remaining ¼ cup sugar until smooth. Set aside.

3. Unfold one sheet of puff pastry dough on a lightly floured
    surface. Use a rolling pin to gently smooth out any cracks. Cut
    the dough into 5 stars and arrange them on one of the prepared
    baking sheets, spacing them 2 inches apart. If needed, gather and
    reroll the dough as you work. Repeat the steps with the remaining
    sheet of dough.

4. In a small bowl, stir together the remaining egg and 1 tablespoon
    water. With an adult's help, use a paring knife to make score lines
    around the center of each star. Use the lines as a guide to add a
    heaping tablespoon of the cream cheese filling to each star. Top
    each with a few berry slices, as shown. Brush the arms of the
    stars with the egg wash.

5. Place the stars in the oven and bake until golden brown,
    about 12 to 15 minutes. Let cool slightly
    before serving.

Purr-fect French Toast

This French toast incorporates one of the Aristocats' favorite treats: cream! Dusted with confectioners' sugar and cinnamon, this is a *meowgical* breakfast.

Directions

1. In a baking dish, whisk together the eggs plus egg yolk, cream, sugar, orange zest, vanilla, and 1 teaspoon cinnamon. In a small bowl, stir together the butter and oil. In another small bowl, stir together the confectioners' sugar and the remaining ¼ teaspoon cinnamon.

2. Coat 3 slices of the bread with the egg mixture. Ask an adult for help with the stove, then warm a large nonstick skillet over medium heat. Brush the skillet with the butter mixture and add the bread slices. Cook on each side until golden, about 3 minutes per side. Transfer to a plate. Repeat with the other 3 slices of bread, adding more butter mixture to the skillet.

3. Lightly dust the toast slices with the cinnamon sugar. Serve immediately with maple syrup.

Makes 6 slices

Ingredients

2 eggs plus 1 egg yolk

½ cup heavy cream

1 Tbsp sugar

¼ tsp orange zest

½ tsp vanilla extract

1¼ tsp ground cinnamon, divided

2 Tbsp melted butter

1 Tbsp vegetable oil

1 Tbsp confectioners' sugar

6 slices brioche or challah bread, cut ¾-inch thick

Maple syrup, for serving

Tip

To reheat leftover French toast, warm it in a nonstick skillet over medium heat until warmed through, about 2 minutes per side.

Makes 4

Ingredients

Flour, for dusting

1 lb pizza dough, divided into 4 portions

¼ cup pizza sauce

¾ cup shredded cheddar cheese

8 slices cooked bacon, chopped

4 eggs

4 tsp chopped fresh chives

Tip

Sometimes cracking eggs takes practice! Ask an adult for help if you want a little guidance on making sure the eggs land in the pizzas' centers.

New York City Breakfast Pizzettes

Joe loves to improvise with whatever he has on hand to create new dishes. This recipe combines two New York City classics—pizza and a bacon, egg, and cheese bagel—into one irresistible dish! Make just one for yourself on a busy holiday morning or use a whole batch of dough to feed a crowd.

Directions

1. Ask an adult for help with the oven. Line two baking sheets with parchment paper and heat the oven to 500°F. On a lightly floured surface, roll each portion of dough into a ¼-inch-thick oval and transfer two to each prepared baking sheet.

2. Top each portion of dough with 1 tablespoon pizza sauce, spreading it and leaving a 1-inch border. Evenly divide the cheddar and bacon among the pizzas. Carefully crack an egg in the center of each pizza.

3. Place the pizzas in the oven and bake until the crust is dark in spots and the egg is cooked through, about 12 to 15 minutes. Let cool slightly, and sprinkle with chives before serving.

Lunch

Sweet Dough Turnovers

Makes 4

Tiana loves discovering her friends' favorite foods. Like stockings, these turnovers are stuffed with treats, and they are perfect for sharing during the holidays—plus you can customize the filling for each of your friends!

Directions

1. In a small bowl, whisk together the flour, baking powder, and salt, and set aside.

2. Using a handheld mixer, cream together the butter and sugar until the mixture is light and fluffy, about 3 minutes. Add the vanilla and the egg and mix to combine. Alternate mixing in a little of the flour mixture with a little of the milk until both are combined. Transfer the dough to a sheet of plastic wrap, roll it up, and place it in the refrigerator for 15 minutes.

3. Ask an adult for help with the oven. Preheat the oven to 375°F. Combine the ingredients for your preferred filling in a small bowl. Remove the dough from the refrigerator and separate into 4 pieces. On a floured surface, roll the dough out into 4 circles with a rolling pin. You can use the mouth of a small bowl to cut out perfect circles, or leave them as they are for a more homemade look.

4. Using a spoon, scoop a fourth of the filling into the center of each small circle. Add water to the edges of the dough, fold the circle in half, and crimp the edges together with a fork.

5. Place on a baking sheet, and bake for 12 to 15 minutes or until golden brown on the outside. Once the turnovers are done, make sure to let them cool down before taking a bite!

Ingredients

Sweet Dough

1 cup plus 2 Tbsp flour

½ tsp baking powder

¼ tsp salt

3 Tbsp unsalted butter, softened

1 Tbsp sugar

¼ tsp vanilla extract

1 Tbsp beaten egg

2 Tbsp milk

Sweet Potato Filling

1 (15-oz) can yams in syrup, drained and mashed

¼ tsp cinnamon

¼ tsp nutmeg

¼ tsp ginger

Broccoli and Cheese Filling

1 cup broccoli, cooked

½ cup cheddar cheese, shredded

1 cup cooked chicken or ham, cubed (optional)

• • •

Makes 8

Ingredients

½ tsp kosher salt

2 Tbsp plus 1 tsp
vegetable oil, divided

1 cup masarepa flour

1 cup shredded
mozzarella cheese

Tip

*Arepas are a treat by
themselves, but you can also
eat them topped with a little
butter, cheese, or even an
egg or avocado.*

Arepas de Queso

Cooking at Casita often becomes a family affair for the
Madrigals! Arepas, made with corn flour and similar to
tortillas, are perfect to cook with your own family—especially
if you're feeding hungry holiday visitors.

Directions

1. In a bowl, blend 1 cup warm water with the salt and 1 teaspoon
    oil. Add masarepa flour and cheese and stir to form a smooth
    dough. Let rest 10 minutes.

2. Evenly divide the dough into 8 portions and roll each into a ball.
    Flatten each ball into a ½-inch-thick disk.

3. Ask an adult for help with the stove, then warm a large cast-iron
    skillet over low heat. Use a heat-safe basting brush to coat the
    bottom of the pan with some of the remaining oil. Add half the
    arepas and cook until dark in spots, about 8 minutes. Flip and
    continue to cook until well browned on the other side. Repeat
    with more oil and the remaining dough. Serve immediately.

Rapunzel's Pumpkin Hazelnut Soup

Hazelnut soup is Rapunzel's favorite dish any time of year, but there's nothing more perfect after a long day of wrapping gifts than this pumpkin version topped with crispy hazelnut bread crumbs.

Directions

1. Ask for an adult's help with the stove. Warm the olive oil in a large pot over medium heat. Once the oil begins to simmer, add the shallot and salt. Cook, stirring occasionally, until the shallot becomes tender and translucent, about 7 to 8 minutes.

2. Add the chicken or vegetable stock, applesauce, pepper, nutmeg, pumpkin puree, and brown sugar, and simmer for 15 minutes. Add the sour cream and stir to combine.

3. For the topping, heat the oil in a small pan over medium heat and add the bread crumbs. Stir them around until they're crisp and golden, about 3 minutes. Pour in the hazelnuts, and toast everything together for 2 minutes. Top each bowl of soup with a tablespoon of bread-crumb topping.

Serves 4 to 6

Ingredients

Pumpkin Soup

1 Tbsp olive oil

1 shallot, diced

½ tsp salt

3 cups chicken or vegetable stock

1 cup unsweetened applesauce

¼ tsp pepper

⅛ tsp nutmeg

1 (15-oz) can pumpkin puree

2 Tbsp brown sugar

½ cup sour cream

Hazelnut Bread-Crumb Topping

½ Tbsp olive oil

¼ cup panko bread crumbs

¼ cup hazelnuts, chopped

Serves 6

Ingredients

3 cups elbow macaroni (plain or whole wheat)

1 Tbsp olive oil

2 Tbsp butter, melted

3 Tbsp flour

1½ cups milk

2 cups white cheddar cheese, shredded

1 cup mozzarella cheese, shredded

¼ tsp ground nutmeg

¼ tsp ground cayenne pepper

1¾ tsp salt

2 cups cauliflower, cooked and chopped

Grated Parmesan cheese, for serving (optional)

Tip

If you'd like a crispy top, pour the entire mixture into a baking dish, cover with an additional 1 cup of mozzarella cheese, and have an adult help you place it in the broiler until it has browned, for about 3 minutes.

Joyful Mac & Cheese

Nothing makes Joy happier than Riley's favorite comfort foods—except maybe celebrating Christmas! This spin on mac and cheese will bring a smile to everyone's face.

Directions

1. Cook the macaroni according to the directions on the box.

2. Ask an adult for help with the stove. Add the oil, butter, and flour to a large pot over medium-low heat, and whisk together for 3 minutes. While continuing to whisk, slowly add in the milk and gently bring to a boil. Stir in the cheddar and mozzarella cheeses one handful at a time. Season with nutmeg, cayenne pepper, and salt.

3. Add the cooked pasta and cauliflower to the pot and stir to coat with the cheese sauce. Garnish with Parmesan cheese before serving, if desired.

Lunar New Year Dumplings

Once Christmas is over, Mei and her family start preparing for Lunar New Year. The holiday is filled with delicious foods like dumplings, which represent wealth for the new year. Mei's father shows her how to make this kind of scrumptious treat.

Directions

1. In a medium bowl, stir together the pork, ginger, garlic, sesame oil, scallions, soy sauce, and white pepper. Line a plate with a paper towel and fill a small bowl with water.

2. Fill a dumpling wrapper with 1 tablespoon of filling and use your finger to dampen the edges with water. Fold the dumpling in half and press together the edges to seal. Repeat with the remaining filling and wrappers.

3. Ask an adult for help with the stove. Warm 1 tablespoon vegetable oil in a large nonstick skillet over medium heat. Add half the dumplings and cook until beginning to brown on the underside, about 3 minutes. Carefully add 3 tablespoons water to the pan, cover, and let steam until the water evaporates, about 3 minutes more. Transfer to the prepared plate and repeat with the remaining dumplings.

4. Serve immediately with soy sauce.

Makes about 1½ to 2 dozen

Ingredients

½ lb ground pork

¾ tsp grated ginger

1 clove garlic, grated

1 tsp sesame oil

2 scallions, chopped

2 tsp soy sauce, plus more for serving

¼ tsp white pepper

24 dumpling wrappers

2 Tbsp vegetable oil

Tip

For instructions on how to do a traditional dumpling fold, turn to page 132.

Ingredients

2 cups green beans,
sliced and cooked

1 (10-oz) can cream
of mushroom soup

¼ cup milk

½ tsp salt

½ tsp pepper

1 tsp garlic powder

1⅓ cups French fried
onions, divided

1 cup cheddar cheese,
shredded

Tip

*This casserole pairs
deliciously with other dishes
in this book—like the
Sweet Dough Turnovers
on page 34—to create
a big feast.*

Festive Green Bean Casserole

This classic Southern casserole, ornamented with gooey cheese, would fit right in on the holiday menu at Tiana's Palace.

Directions

1. Ask an adult for help with the oven. Preheat the oven to 350°F. In a large bowl, stir together the green beans, mushroom soup, milk, salt, pepper, garlic powder, and ⅔ cup of the French fried onions. Pour into a greased 1½-quart baking dish and bake for 15 minutes.

2. Add the cheddar cheese and the remaining ⅔ cup French fried onions, and bake for another 5 to 10 minutes or until the cheese has melted.

Rapunzel Pizza Braid

Braiding this pizza pocket is as simple as tying a holiday bow. Just as Rapunzel tucks flowers into her festive hairdo, you can decorate this recipe with cheese, pepperoni, and more!

Directions

1. Ask an adult for help with the oven. Heat the oven to 400°F. Line a baking sheet with parchment paper. Remove the dough from the package and place it on the parchment. Use a toothpick to make 2 marks along the short edge of the dough, dividing it into 3 even portions. Then use the toothpick to mark every 1 inch along each long edge. With an adult's help, use a knife or kitchen shears to cut along one long side at the marks you made, stopping when you reach the first mark on the short edge. Then repeat on the other long side. You should end up with strips on both long sides of the dough, with an uncut portion of dough in the middle.

2. Use your hands to crush the tomatoes into small pieces and place them in a bowl. Stir in the garlic and season with salt and pepper. Spread this mix over the center of the dough.

3. Sprinkle on the cheese, followed by the pepperoni. Fold the dough by overlapping the strips, alternating between the two sides.

4. Whisk the egg with 1 tablespoon water. Brush the top of the braid with this egg wash and sprinkle with sesame seeds. Place the pizza in the oven and bake until golden brown, about 25 minutes. Let cool slightly before serving.

• • •

Serves 4 to 6

Ingredients

1 (14-oz) package refrigerated pizza dough

4 tomatoes from a 14-oz can

1 small clove garlic, grated

Kosher salt, to taste

Black pepper, to taste

1¼ cups shredded mozzarella cheese

16 pieces pepperoni

1 egg

1 tsp sesame seeds

Tip

For an easier method for beginner cooks, use kitchen shears in place of a knife to cut strips into the dough.

Makes 8

Ingredients

1 cup uncooked sushi rice

1 Tbsp toasted sesame seeds

3 sheets nori seaweed

3 Tbsp soy sauce

2 Tbsp plus 1 tsp dark brown sugar

1 clove garlic, grated

1 (12-oz) package canned ham, tin rinsed and reserved

1 Tbsp vegetable oil

Tip

Dipping your fingers in water before touching the rice will keep it from sticking to your hands and make handling the musubi much easier.

Ham Musubi

Spread love and cheer to your *'ohana* (which means family) with a tasty snack wrapped just like a package. Each bundle is made with sushi rice, ham, and seaweed, just like the ones Lilo, Stitch, and Nani might eat on the islands of Hawai'i.

Directions

1. Cook the rice according to the package directions. Stir in the sesame seeds. Cut each nori sheet into 3 even strips.

2. In a baking dish, whisk together the soy sauce, brown sugar, and garlic. Carefully cut the ham crosswise into 8 even slices. Place them in the dish with the marinade and coat each slice on both sides.

3. Ask an adult for help with the stove. Warm the oil over medium heat in a large nonstick skillet. Add half the ham slices and cook until dark brown in spots on the underside, about 3 minutes. Flip and cook on the other side for 3 minutes more. Transfer to a plate, then repeat with the remaining ham.

4. To make each musubi, line the ham can with plastic wrap, letting it hang over the edges of the can by a few inches. Add ¼ cup rice, then use the back of a spoon to press it evenly into the bottom of the can. Add a slice of the cooked ham and use the spoon to press it in place. Use the plastic wrap to lift out the ham and rice, then remove the plastic and wrap the bundle with a strip of nori, as shown. Repeat with the remaining rice, ham, and nori sheets. (You'll have one nori sheet left over.)

Dinner

Lady and the Tramp Sheet Pan Meatballs and Sauce

Though Lady and Tramp enjoy their favorite spaghetti and meatball dish year-round, the festive red colors in this version make it the perfect addition to a holiday table.

Directions

To Make the Red Sauce

1. Ask an adult for help with the stove. In a large skillet over medium heat, warm the oil. Add the onion and cook until softened, about 4 minutes. Add the garlic and cook 1 minute. Add the tomatoes, bay leaf, fresh herbs, salt, and pepper, and stir to combine.

2. Bring the sauce to a boil, then reduce the heat and let simmer 10 minutes. Remove from the heat and pluck out the herb stems and bay leaf.

3. Place half the sauce in a blender and puree. Add the puree back to the pan, place over low heat, and stir in the butter. Once butter has melted, remove from the heat, cover, and set aside.

To Make the Meatballs

1. Line a baking sheet with foil and set the broiler to high with a rack 6 inches below the heat. In a large bowl, use your hands to combine the meatball ingredients, and toss until evenly blended. Do not overmix.

2. Scoop a golf-ball-size portion of the meatball mixture and shape it into a ball. Transfer to the prepared baking sheet. Continue with remaining mixture, spacing the meatballs ½ inch apart.

3. Broil the meatballs for 4 minutes, then remove from the oven, flip, and broil 4 minutes more. Serve immediately with sauce and, if you like, your favorite pasta.

Serves 6

Ingredients

Red Sauce

1 Tbsp olive oil

1 large onion, chopped

3 cloves garlic, minced

2 (28-ounce) cans diced tomatoes

1 bay leaf

6 sprigs fresh thyme or oregano

1 tsp kosher salt

½ tsp black pepper

1 Tbsp butter

Meatballs

½ lb ground beef

½ lb ground pork

½ cup panko bread crumbs

¼ cup grated Parmesan cheese

2 eggs

2 tsp chopped fresh oregano

1 tsp chopped fresh parsley

¼ cup finely chopped shallots

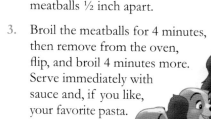

Serves 8

Ingredients

Cooking spray

1 store-bought
refrigerated piecrust

3 scallions, chopped

5 slices cooked bacon,
chopped

¾ cup shredded Jarlsberg
cheese

6 large eggs

1¼ cups heavy cream

¼ teaspoon kosher salt

⅛ teaspoon black pepper

Pinch ground nutmeg

2 large black olives,
halved lengthwise

¼ small red bell pepper

½ small yellow bell pepper

9 fresh chives

2 slices white cheddar

Tip

*For a quick, time-saving riff
on this recipe, replace
the bacon with diced deli ham
and use your favorite
shredded cheese in place
of the Jarlsberg.*

Aristocat-ic Quiche Marie

**Kitten Marie knows that the perfect gift for her friend
Roquefort is his favorite food—cheese! You can make your
own cheesy treat to share with friends during the holidays,
based on a classic French recipe called quiche Lorraine.**

Directions

1. Ask an adult for help with the oven. Heat the oven to 350°F.
   Coat a 9-inch pie pan with cooking spray. Place the piecrust in
   the pan and crimp the edges. Scatter the scallions, bacon, and
   cheese in the crust and toss lightly to mix.

2. In a medium bowl, whisk together the eggs, heavy cream, salt,
   pepper, and nutmeg. Pour the mixture over the other filling
   ingredients. Bake until the filling is set in the center and beginning
   to brown in some spots, about 40 minutes. Let cool slightly.

3. To make Marie's face, slice an olive into strips for the mouth.
   Halve the second olive to form two pupils. Cut a bow and nose
   from the red bell pepper and two ears from the yellow bell pepper.
   Trim 6 chives for the whiskers and 3 for the tuft of fur. Use a
   round cutter to cut a circle from each slice of cheddar for the
   eyes. Set all the pieces in place as shown. Serve immediately.

Lightning McQueen's Pot Pie

Decorated with Lightning McQueen's signature lightning bolt, this dish gives you all the fuel you need during the busy holiday season.

Directions

1. Ask an adult for help with the oven. Heat oven to 375°F. Grease 4 small (4½ x 1¼-inch) aluminum pie tins or ovenproof bowls. Cut the 2 piecrusts into 8 individual pieces using the top of the pie tin as a guide. Line the bottom of each tin with 1 piece of crust. Using a small cookie cutter or a knife (with an adult's help), cut out a small lightning bolt in the center of each of the remaining 4 pieces of crust.

2. In a medium bowl, whisk together the soup, milk, and egg. Mix in the vegetables, chicken, salt, pepper, thyme, and nutmeg.

3. Divide the filling among the 4 tins or bowls, cover each with a top crust, and crimp the edges together to seal. Trim any overhang.

4. Carefully place the pies in the oven, and bake until golden brown, 30 to 40 minutes. Let cool for 10 minutes before serving.

Serves 4

Ingredients

2 9-inch store-bought piecrusts, thawed

1 (10½-oz) can condensed cream of chicken soup

½ cup milk

1 egg, lightly beaten

1 (8-oz) package frozen mixed vegetables, thawed

1 cup chicken, cubed and cooked

1 tsp salt

¼ tsp pepper

¼ tsp thyme

¼ tsp nutmeg

Tip

Leave out the chicken and substitute condensed cream of potato or mushroom soup for an equally delicious vegetable pie!

Ingredients

1 lb lean ground beef

1 cup onion, chopped

1 (14½-oz) can stewed
or roasted tomatoes

1 (8-oz) can tomato
sauce

1 (15-oz) can dark red
kidney beans, drained

1 (15-oz) can light red
kidney beans, drained

1 (14-oz) can beef broth

2 tsp garlic powder

1 tsp salt

½ tsp pepper

Tip

*Want to enjoy leftovers
the next day? Place a bowl
of chili in the microwave
and heat for one minute.
With an adult's help,
stir the chili and continue
to microwave in
one-minute bursts until
heated through.*

Woody's Cowboy Chili

You don't have to be a cowboy to enjoy a delicious bowl of chili, but this hearty dish will make you feel as cheerful as Woody and his friends do while welcoming new toys into their family on Christmas.

Directions

1. Ask an adult for help with the stove. Place the beef and onion in a large pot and cook them over medium-high heat until the meat is brown and the onions are tender.

2. Add the remaining ingredients except for the cheddar cheese to the pot. Stir, bring to a boil, and reduce heat to low.

3. Cover partially and let simmer for 30 to 45 minutes (the longer it simmers, the thicker your chili will be). If you'd like, serve with garnishes like parsley or tortilla chips.

To Infinity and Beyond Meat Loaf

Buzz Lightyear takes pride in building his snow Space Rangers. And every Space Ranger needs a rocket ship to travel to the moon and back! After a long day of holiday fun, you can come back down to Earth with this tasty meat loaf that represents Buzz's out-of-this-world adventures.

Directions

To Make the Sauce

1. Mix together the ketchup and Worcestershire sauce in a small bowl and set aside.

To Make the Meat Loaf

1. Ask an adult for help with the oven. Preheat the oven to 350°F. Line a 9 x 13-inch baking pan with aluminum foil, then spray with cooking spray and set aside.

2. Combine all of the remaining meat loaf ingredients in a large bowl with your hands. Scoop out a handful of the meat mixture, and form it into a rocket shape on the baking sheet, adding more of the mixture for each wing.

3. Place the pan in the oven, and bake for 40 to 50 minutes. Carefully remove the sheet and let it sit for 5 minutes before moving the meat loaves to a plate. Decorate each loaf with the sauce and serve.

Serves 6

Ingredients

Sauce

¼ cup ketchup

4 tsp Worcestershire sauce

Meat Loaf

Cooking spray

¼ cup ketchup

½ small onion, minced

1 tsp olive oil

1 lb ground turkey or beef

½ cup bread crumbs

1 egg

½ tsp oregano

½ tsp basil

1 tsp salt

¼ tsp pepper

½ of a small zucchini, grated (optional)

½ of a carrot, peeled and grated (optional)

• • •

Serves 4

Ingredients

¼ cup chopped basil

1 medium zucchini, sliced into ½-inch-thick semicircles

1 medium yellow squash, sliced into ½-inch-thick semicircles

1 small eggplant, cut into 1-inch cubes

4 smoked pork sausages, sliced into thirds

¾ tsp smoked paprika

1 cup cherry tomatoes, halved

6 baby bell peppers, trimmed and quartered

2 Tbsp olive oil

½ tsp kosher salt

1 tsp herbes de Provence

Tip

For an extra flavor boost, you can also top this dish with chopped fresh parsley, a squeeze of lemon, or a sprinkle of feta or Parmesan cheese.

Sheet Pan Ratatouille with Smoked Sausage

Christmas is a busy season at Remy's restaurant, but he always takes time to share a special meal with his family and friends. The bright colors in this simple version of Remy's signature dish make it a festive addition to your table.

Directions

1. Ask an adult for help with the oven. Heat the oven to 425°F. Line two baking sheets with parchment paper.

2. Toss half the basil and the remaining ingredients in a large bowl. Distribute evenly among the baking sheets. Do not crowd the pans. Roast, stirring once, until the vegetables begin to caramelize and char slightly, about 25 minutes. Serve immediately topped with the remaining basil.

Merida's Day-After-Christmas Sliders

Merida's triplet brothers always like to play, but never more than on the day after Christmas! Reuse Christmas dinner leftovers to make these delicious turkey sliders, which, in the triplets' honor, can be customized with three toppings.

Directions

1. Prepare the stuffing according to the package instructions. Keep warm until ready to serve, or reheat in the microwave before serving.

2. In a medium bowl, combine the ground turkey, bread crumbs, onion powder, garlic, salt, and pepper. Use this mixture to form eight 3-inch-wide patties.

3. Ask an adult for help with the stove. Spray a large pan with cooking spray, and heat it over medium heat. Add the patties, and cook until browned, about 5 minutes per side. Remove from the pan.

4. Warm the gravy in the microwave. Spread cranberry sauce on one side of the buns. Place the patties on the buns, mound a small amount of stuffing on each, and top with the gravy.

Makes 12

Ingredients

Sliders

1 lb lean ground turkey

¼ cup bread crumbs

2 tsp onion powder

1 clove garlic, crushed

1 tsp kosher salt

½ tsp ground pepper

Cooking spray

12 whole wheat slider rolls

Toppings

1 package stuffing

1 jar turkey or chicken gravy

1 (12-oz) can cranberry sauce

Tip

Play around with the topping combinations for these sliders! For example, if you're craving more stuffing, you can leave the other toppings out.

Serves 8

Ingredients

12 oz bow tie pasta

1 tsp olive oil

5 oz pepperoni, sliced

1 bunch curly green kale, chopped

1 (24-oz) jar marinara sauce

Grated Parmesan cheese, for serving

Tip

This recipe works best with stick pepperoni, which you can hand cut thicker than precut pepperoni. The latter will cook more quickly, so watch carefully if you use it.

Pinocchio's Pepperoni Pasta

Around Christmas, Pinocchio wears his most festive attire, including his signature bow tie. Featuring a matching pasta shape, this namesake dish is full of Christmas color.

Directions

1. Ask an adult for help with the stove. Boil the pasta according to the package directions and then drain, reserving ½ cup pasta water.

2. Warm the oil in a large, high-sided nonstick skillet over medium heat. Add the pepperoni and cook until lightly browned, about 3 minutes. Add half the kale and cook, stirring occasionally, until beginning to wilt. Add the remaining kale and continue to cook until fully wilted, about 3 minutes more. Add the sauce, reduce the heat to low, and let simmer 5 minutes.

3. Stir in the pasta and ¼ cup of the reserved pasta water. Continue to cook, gently tossing the pasta with tongs, until it is coated and the water has evaporated, about 2 minutes. If the pasta dries out quickly, you can add another 1 or 2 tablespoons of pasta water to loosen it. Top with Parmesan cheese, if desired, and serve immediately.

Pork Tenderloin Planks with Green Herb Sauce

• • •

Serves 8

The rich green color of the Darling children's beloved Christmas tree reminds them of their adventures in Never Land alongside Peter Pan and Tinker Bell. This main dish features an irresistible sauce made with fresh herbs and lemon that captures some of those magical green hues, too.

Directions

1. Ask an adult for help with the oven, then heat it to 400°F. Place the olive oil, salt, pepper, cilantro, mint, basil, lemon juice, and garlic in a food processor. Blend until smooth. Transfer 3 tablespoons of the sauce to a small bowl and set the rest aside for serving.

2. Season the tenderloins with salt and pepper. Use the 3 tablespoons of sauce to baste them, then place them on a baking sheet. Roast until a thermometer inserted in the center of each registers 145°F, about 25 minutes. With an adult's help, place the pan under the broiler for 1 to 2 minutes to lightly brown the outsides of the roasts. Watch carefully to avoid burning. Let rest 5 minutes, then serve with the remaining sauce.

Ingredients

6 Tbsp olive oil

½ tsp kosher salt, plus extra for seasoning

¼ tsp black pepper, plus extra for seasoning

1½ packed cups cilantro leaves and tender stems

2 packed Tbsp torn fresh mint

¼ cup torn fresh basil leaves

1 to 2 Tbsp lemon juice

1 clove garlic

2 small (1-lb) pork tenderloins, trimmed

Tip

The sauce in this recipe can be made a day ahead and refrigerated.
If it becomes solid overnight, be sure to give it enough time to reach room temperature before using.

69

Serves 4

Ingredients

²⁄₃ cup flour, divided

1 Tbsp kosher salt,
plus more for seasoning

1 tsp black pepper, plus
more for seasoning

2 large (1½-lb)
boneless skinless
chicken breasts

3 Tbsp butter, divided

2 Tbsp olive oil, divided

1 clove garlic, sliced

1 small shallot, chopped

1 cup, plus 2 Tbsp
chicken broth

¾ tsp lemon zest

2 Tbsp lemon juice

3 Tbsp capers

1 Tbsp fresh chopped
parsley (optional)

Tip

*The parsley sprinkled on
at the end of the dish
adds a delicious layer of
flavor, but it can also be
omitted or replaced with
chives or cilantro.*

Magic Hammer Chicken

Fix-It Felix Jr.'s magic hammer comes in handy when decorating for the holidays. Power up with a smashingly good meal that will give you enough energy to trim your tree, wrap a few gifts, and maybe even sing a few carols.

Directions

1. Set aside 1 teaspoon of the flour in a small bowl. Place the remaining flour in a small baking dish and stir in the salt and pepper.

2. With an adult's help, halve each chicken breast crosswise. Place one of the pieces between two sheets of parchment paper and use a meat mallet to flatten it until it is ¼-inch thick. Repeat with the remaining chicken.

3. Place the chicken on a plate and season each portion on both sides with salt and pepper. Place the pieces in the flour mixture and toss to coat them.

4. Ask an adult for help with the stove. In a large, heavy skillet over medium heat, warm 1 tablespoon each of the butter and olive oil. Once melted and bubbly, place 2 portions of the chicken in the pan. Cook until golden on the underside, about 4 minutes. Flip and continue to cook until golden and cooked through, about 4 minutes more. Transfer the chicken to a paper towel–lined plate, cover with foil, and repeat with the remaining chicken, adding 1 tablespoon each of butter and oil to the pan.

5. To the same pan, add the garlic and shallot and cook 1 minute. Add the remaining butter and reserved teaspoon of flour and cook 1 minute more. Add the broth and let simmer until thickened, about 3 minutes. Stir in the lemon zest, lemon juice, and capers, then place the chicken back in the pan to coat and warm through. Transfer the chicken and sauce to a platter and sprinkle with parsley, if desired. Serve immediately.

Sides

Wreck-It Ralph's Smashed Potatoes

Channel your inner Ralph and have fun smashing these roasted potatoes to make an easy side for any holiday meal.

Directions

1. Ask an adult for help with the stove. Fill a large pot with water, add about 1 teaspoon of salt, and then add the potatoes. Set the pot over high heat until the water begins to boil, and then turn the heat down to medium-low and let it simmer for about 20 minutes, or until the potatoes feel soft when you insert a fork.

2. Ask an adult for help with the oven. Preheat the oven to 450°F. While the potatoes cook, line a baking pan with aluminum foil and coat it with cooking spray. Once an adult has carefully removed the potatoes from the water, arrange them on the pan so that they are evenly spaced.

3. Using the bottom of a glass, press down on each potato to smash it. Once all the potatoes are smashed, drizzle them with olive oil and season with salt and pepper.

4. Place the baking pan on the top rack of the oven, and roast the potatoes for 20 to 25 minutes or until crispy and brown at the edges. Remove from the oven and let them cool down before you enjoy them!

Serves 4

Ingredients

2 tsp kosher salt, divided

12 small potatoes (such as red bliss)

Cooking spray

½ cup extra-virgin olive oil

Ground pepper, to taste

Tip

If you're short on time, you can boil and smash these potatoes the night before and store them in the refrigerator. The next day, just let the potatoes reach room temperature before placing them in the oven.

Ingredients

4 medium apples, peeled
(McIntosh or Granny
Smith work best)

½ cup light brown sugar

1 tsp ground cinnamon

¼ tsp ground nutmeg

4 Tbsp water

1 Tbsp butter

Tip

*If the glaze becomes too
thick, thin it by adding
a tablespoon of water
at a time until it is the
right consistency.*

Snow White's Cinnamon Apples

Snow White's iconic apples get a wintry twist in this spice-filled side dish. It comes together in around 15 minutes, leaving plenty of time for other holiday activities.

Directions

1. Carefully slice apples with an apple slicer. In a medium bowl, toss together apples, light brown sugar, cinnamon, and nutmeg.

2. Ask an adult for help with the stove. Put apple mixture, water, and butter into a medium saucepan, and cook it over medium heat, stirring occasionally, until apples are tender, 14 to 16 minutes.

Chicken Long Rice

This popular dish is a mainstay at many Hawaiian luaus, including the one that Lilo and Stitch host each Christmas. It's a cinch to make and so delightful it could even star as an entrée.

Directions

1. Ask an adult for help with the stove. Combine the broth, ginger, garlic, and scallion whites in a large pot over medium heat. Bring to a simmer. Add the chicken and continue to cook, partially covered, until the chicken is cooked through, about 12 minutes.

2. With an adult's help, transfer the chicken from the pot to a cutting board. Reduce the heat beneath the pot to low and add the mung bean noodles. Cook 3 minutes, then cover and turn off the heat.

3. Use two forks to shred the chicken into small pieces. Add it back to the pot. Serve the noodles, chicken, and broth hot, with scallion greens scattered on top.

Serves 6

Ingredients

6 cups chicken broth

2-inch piece fresh ginger, peeled and sliced

2 cloves garlic, smashed

4 scallions, whites and greens separated and sliced

4 small chicken thighs

4 oz mung bean (also known as glass) noodles

Tip

To streamline this recipe, you can purchase frozen, precut ginger. You'll need about 2 scant teaspoons for this recipe.

Serves 4

Ingredients

4 Persian cucumbers,
trimmed

½ cup halved cherry or
grape tomatoes

4 tsp chopped fresh dill

½ small red onion, sliced

1 Tbsp apple cider vinegar

1 clove garlic, grated

2 Tbsp olive oil

½ tsp kosher salt

¼ tsp black pepper

½ tsp honey

Tip

*For instructions on how
to cut the vegetables
with a peeler,* *turn to page 133.*

Christmas Ribbon Salad

Want to become an expert chef like Remy? Give an ordinary cucumber salad the four-star holiday treatment by using a vegetable peeler to cut the cucumber into fanciful ribbons, like those used to deck the halls.

Directions

1. Carefully use a vegetable peeler to slice the cucumbers into thin strips. Place them in a medium bowl with the tomatoes, dill, and onion.

2. In a small bowl, whisk together the vinegar, garlic, olive oil, salt, pepper, and honey. Pour the dressing over the vegetables and toss to coat. Serve immediately.

Dreamy Winter Slaw

When snow covers the fairies' vegetable garden, Aurora feels like she's waltzing through a wintry dreamland. Here, leafy greens and brussels sprouts are dressed in citrus and stirred together with tart pomegranate seeds for a tasty salad that brings the same magic to your table.

Directions

1. In a small bowl, whisk together the lemon juice, mustard, olive oil, salt, and pepper. In a large bowl, combine the kale, brussels sprouts, almonds, and pomegranate seeds. Add the dressing and toss to coat. Just before serving, top the salad with Parmesan cheese.

Serves 8

Ingredients

4 tsp lemon juice

2 Tbsp Dijon mustard

4 Tbsp olive oil

1½ tsp kosher salt

¼ tsp black pepper

½ small bunch curly green kale, thinly sliced

12 oz brussels sprouts, trimmed and thinly sliced

¼ cup toasted almonds, roughly chopped

¼ cup pomegranate seeds

¼ cup grated Parmesan cheese

Tip

When shopping for this recipe, look for the biggest brussels sprouts you can find. They will be easier to prep and cut.

Snacks

Ingredients

4 small bananas, halved crosswise

1 cup white chocolate chips

2 Tbsp coconut oil

⅓ cup dark chocolate chips

Special Equipment

8 wooden sticks

Tip

Be sure to use coconut oil for the recipe. Other oils won't set properly.

Frozen Banana Dalmatian Pops

Brrr! One bite of this sweet spotted snack and you'll want to cuddle up inside like the Dalmatians!

Directions

1. Line a small baking sheet with parchment paper. Insert a wooden stick into the flat side of each banana and place it on the sheet. Freeze the bananas until solid, about 3 hours.

2. Ask an adult for help with the stove or microwave, and melt the white chocolate according to the package directions. Add the coconut oil and whisk until melted. Transfer to a mug or tall glass.

3. Dip each banana in the white chocolate, letting the excess drip off, then return it to the baking sheet. Melt the chocolate chips according to the package directions. Place in a piping bag fit with an extra-small writing tip. Pipe spots onto each banana pop, then return the pops to the freezer until ready to serve. If you prefer, you can simply use the chocolate chips from the bag and place them onto the white chocolate. Like sprinkles, the spots will fall off easily, so take care when eating!

Ariel's Starfish Dip

These sea-inspired mouthfuls, decorated with festive green, red, and gold pepper stars, are especially yummy after a busy day of wrapping presents or playing in the snow.

Directions

1. Squeeze the spinach to remove any excess water. Put the spinach, mayonnaise, onion soup mix, and sour cream into a large bowl and combine.

2. Using the back of a small spoon, smear about a teaspoon of dip onto one side of a cucumber round. Arrange 5 pieces of pepper on top to give the appearance of a starfish or Christmas star, and serve.

Serves 6

Ingredients

1 (10-oz) package frozen spinach, thawed

½ cup low-fat mayonnaise

1 package onion soup mix

1 (8-oz) container low-fat sour cream

2 cucumbers, sliced into 1-inch rounds

½ red pepper, cut into 1-inch-thick strips and then sliced on the diagonal

½ green pepper, cut into 1-inch-thick strips and then sliced on the diagonal

½ yellow pepper, cut into 1-inch-thick strips and then sliced on the diagonal

Tip

Feeling adventurous? Try putting this dip on top of other veggies and snacks, too!

Aurora's Yummy Yogurt Dip

After a long day of pulling a sleigh over fields of snow, Aurora treats Samson to his favorite snack—carrots! You can enjoy them too alongside this refreshing yogurt dip.

* * *

Serves 2 to 3

Ingredients

1 (5⅓-oz) container of plain Greek yogurt

½ Tbsp freshly squeezed lemon juice

½ tsp dried oregano

¼ tsp salt

Pinch of ground pepper

3 large carrots, peeled and cut into sticks

Tip

Carrots aren't the only veggie you can dunk into this tasty dip. It's also good with celery, cucumber slices, cherry tomatoes, and broccoli.

Directions

1. Combine the yogurt, lemon juice, oregano, salt, and pepper in a small bowl and mix with a spoon. Serve alongside the carrots.

Peanut Butter Puppy Chow

Lady, Tramp, and their puppies are a big part of all their human family's holiday celebrations. This sweet, salty twist on a puppy chow snack mix makes for a special holiday treat—and while the ingredients aren't safe for animals to eat, chomping on these will remind you of how important your furry friends are to celebrating!

Directions

1. Line a baking sheet with parchment paper. Place the sugar in a gallon-sized resealable plastic bag and place the cereal in a large bowl.

2. In a microwave-safe bowl or liquid measuring cup, combine the chocolate chips, peanut butter, and butter. Ask an adult for help with the microwave, then heat the mixture in the microwave at 50 percent power for 1 minute. Carefully but vigorously stir to melt the chocolate, then continue to heat in 10-second bursts, stirring between each, until fully melted.

3. Pour the chocolate mixture over the cereal. Use a rubber spatula to gently stir together the ingredients until the cereal is evenly coated. Let sit 3 minutes, then transfer to the bag with the sugar and seal the bag.

4. Shake the cereal in the sugar until fully coated. Pour out onto the prepared baking sheet and shake to spread out (don't use your hands, as the coating will not be set). Let cool 20 minutes, then combine in a bowl with the chocolate candies and pretzels. Serve right away or store in a resealable plastic bag up to three days.

Makes about 6 cups

Ingredients

¾ cup confectioners' sugar

4 cups square rice cereal

½ cup semisweet chocolate chips

¼ cup peanut butter

1 Tbsp unsalted butter

¾ cup chocolate pastel candies

1 cup mini pretzel twists

Tip

Mini pretzels are the perfect size for this treat, but if you can't find them, you can substitute larger twists or nuggets or another shape.

Makes 2 wreaths

Ingredients

2 mini red bell peppers

2 mini yellow
bell peppers

1 mini bagel

3 Tbsp cream cheese,
softened

4 large broccoli florets,
cut into ½-inch pieces

Tip

*For instructions on how
to cut the veggies with
a straw for this recipe,
turn to page 134.*

Hoppy Holidays Garden Veggie Wreath

What's better than a wreath made of beautiful sweet-smelling pine branches and ruby red berries? An edible one fashioned with the most favored food group in Zootopia—vegetables!

Directions

1. Cut the red and yellow peppers into halves, then use a mini round cutter to cut the red peppers into circles. Set aside. Use the end of a straw to cut circles from each of the yellow bell peppers.

2. Cover each half of the bagel with 1 tablespoon cream cheese. Arrange the broccoli on top of each bagel half as shown. Use a toothpick and the remaining cream cheese to attach red and yellow bell pepper baubles to each. Eat immediately.

Beverages

Never Land Hot Chocolate with Star Marshmallows

To get to Never Land, you must fly toward the second star to the right. This hot chocolate is topped with a marshmallow inspired by that very same star.

Directions

To Make the Star Marshmallows

1. Fill a small bowl with ½ cup cold water and sprinkle the gelatin on top. Let sit 10 minutes. Line a 9 x 13-inch baking pan with plastic wrap and coat it with cooking spray.

2. Ask an adult with for help with the stove. In a large saucepan over medium heat, combine the granulated sugar with ½ cup water and stir until the sugar is dissolved. Add the gelatin mix and bring to a boil. Remove from the heat and carefully pour the mixture into a large bowl. Let cool slightly. Add the salt and vanilla, and beat with a hand mixer until soft peaks form, about 10 to 15 minutes. Pour the mixture into the prepared pan and spread evenly with an oiled spatula. Set it aside until firm, about 3 hours.

3. Flip the marshmallows out of the pan and remove the plastic. Cover the top with sprinkles, then cut into stars with an oiled cookie cutter. Dust the bottom and edges of each star with confectioners' sugar.

To Make the Cocoa

1. Whisk together the cocoa powder, sugar, salt, and ¼ cup of the milk in a saucepan over low heat. Warm, stirring occasionally, until the cocoa and sugar dissolve. Add the remining milk and heat, whisking constantly, until hot. Divide among 4 mugs and top each with 1 or 2 marshmallows.

Serves 4

Ingredients

Star Marshmallows

2 ½ cups of water, divided

2 Tbsp (2 packets) gelatin

Cooking spray

2 cups granulated sugar

¼ tsp salt

2 tsp vanilla extract

2 Tbsp silver sprinkles

¾ cup confectioners' sugar

Cooking oil

Cocoa

½ cup unsweetened cocoa powder

½ cup sugar

Pinch of salt

1 quart your favorite milk, divided

Special Equipment

Small star-shaped cookie cutter

Tip

If you'd like, you can try a variety of cookie-cutter shapes on the marshmallows.

Serves 2

Ingredients

Whipped Cream

½ cup heavy cream

½ tsp vanilla extract

½ Tbsp confectioners' sugar

Milkshake

4 to 6 scoops of your favorite mint chocolate chip ice cream

¼ cup whole milk

6 chocolate sandwich cookies

Tip

Want to make sure the whipped cream swirl atop the milkshake looks just like the photo? Try using a piping bag! Check out page 86 for more info.

Jiminy Cricket Milkshake

Jiminy Cricket is the perfect tree-decorating helper because he's small enough to climb it and place the star at the top. This milkshake evokes a classic winter flavor—peppermint—and is the perfect reminder that even a small dose of flavor can go a long way.

Directions

1. Leave the ice cream out on the counter for about 10 minutes to soften.

To Make the Whipped Cream

1. Add the heavy cream to a medium bowl. With a handheld whisk or electric mixer with a whisk attachment, whip the cream until it begins to thicken (so when you lift the whisk from the bowl, the cream should stick slightly to the whisk and then fall over).

2. Add the vanilla extract and sugar to the bowl, and continue whisking until the cream's peaks can stand up on their own. Be careful not to over-whisk!

To Make the Milkshake

1. Blend the softened ice cream, milk, and 4 cookies in a blender until combined. Pour into two glasses and top each with the whipped cream. Crumble the remaining 2 cookies and sprinkle on top, as shown in the photo.

Aunt Cass's Apple Cider

Hiro's aunt Cass always makes sure her family feels special and loved, especially during the holidays. Capture that warmth and Christmas cheer with this cozy drink, made with apple cider, oranges, and spices, and enjoy it with your own family throughout the winter season.

Directions

1. Ask an adult for help at the stove. In a medium saucepan, combine the cider, cinnamon sticks, orange slices, star anise, and cloves. Warm over medium heat until the mixture begins to bubble around the edges. Reduce the heat to low and simmer 20 minutes. Turn off the heat and let sit 5 minutes more. Stir in the honey, if using.

2. Set a mesh strainer over a bowl. With an adult's help, pour the cider through the strainer and discard the solids. Pour the cider into mugs and garnish each with a cinnamon stick and an orange slice. Serve warm.

Serves 4

Ingredients

4 cups apple cider

2 cinnamon sticks, plus more for garnish

6 orange slices, plus more for garnish

4 star anise pods

4 whole cloves

1 Tbsp honey (optional)

Tip

Letting the mixture steep for several minutes after the cider simmers will add more flavor.

Ingredients

1½ cups whole milk

½ cup heavy cream

½ cup cream of coconut

4 large eggs

1 (16-oz) can
pineapple juice

¼ cup brown sugar

2 tsp vanilla extract

½ tsp ground cinnamon

¼ tsp nutmeg

⅛ tsp ground cloves

4 pineapple wedges
(optional)

Tip

*To add another tropical twist,
you can also garnish
with decorations like
the mini umbrella shown
in the photo.*

Stitch's Hawaiian Eggnog

**Transport yourself to the islands Lilo and Stitch call home
with this creamy Hawaiian twist on this signature holiday
drink!**

Directions

1. Add the milk, cream, cream of coconut, eggs, pineapple juice,
   and brown sugar to a large pot and whisk to combine.

2. Ask an adult for help with the stove. Heat the mixture over low
   heat, whisking constantly, until it thickens slightly (about 10 to 15
   minutes). Do not let it boil.

3. Remove the pot from the heat and stir in the vanilla extract and
   spices. Garnish with a pineapple wedge, if desired, and serve
   immediately.

Agua de Jamaica

This sweet and tart drink is popular in Miguel's homeland of Mexico all year-round, but its crimson color makes it perfect for the Christmas season—especially with a festive green garnish like rosemary, or a warming cinnamon stick for stirring.

Directions

1. Ask an adult for help with the stove. Combine the water, sugar, and cinnamon stick in a pot over high heat. Stir occasionally to dissolve the sugar, then bring to a boil. Add the hibiscus, turn off the heat, and let steep 30 minutes. Strain the brew into a pitcher and let cool completely. Just before serving, stir in the lime juice. Serve the drink over ice, and if you'd like, garnish with a cinnamon stick.

Serves 6

Ingredients

6 cups water

¾ cup sugar

1 cinnamon stick, plus extras for garnish (optional)

1¼ cups hibiscus flowers

Juice of ½ a lime

Tip

This drink can be made up to 2 days ahead. Keep it refrigerated until ready to serve.

Sweets

Ingredients

1 lb white chocolate
(chips or bar, chopped)

½ cup candy canes or
starlight mints, crushed

½ cup mini marshmallows

Tip

*It's easy to crush candy canes,
even without a blender.
Just add a few candy canes to
a zip-top bag and crush
them with a rolling pin.*

Sherwood Forest Peppermint Bark

**Robin Hood and his friends have a hard time selecting
a Christmas tree when they have a whole forest to choose
from! Bring a bit of their woodland home into your
kitchen with this white chocolate dessert, knotted with
crushed peppermint and marshmallows.**

Directions

1. Line a 9 x 13-inch baking pan with parchment paper or
    aluminum foil. Set aside.

2. Ask an adult to help you with the microwave. Place the white
    chocolate in a bowl and microwave for 30 seconds. Remove from
    microwave, using caution with the hot bowl, stir the chocolate
    with a spatula, and place it back in the microwave. Continue to
    microwave the chocolate in 30-second intervals, stirring in
    between, until it has all melted.

3. Pour the chocolate into the baking pan and smooth it out with
    the spatula. Quickly sprinkle on the candy cane pieces and
    marshmallows, and lightly press them into the chocolate. Let
    the bark harden for at least an hour at room temperature before
    breaking into pieces.

Dumbo's Big Top Candy Cane Cupcakes

Around Christmastime, the red-and-white circus tent that Dumbo and Timothy call home takes on a festive candy cane appearance. Re-create it with these decorated cupcakes.

Directions

1. Cut a 3-inch length of washi tape. Center and fold the tape over the top of a toothpick, as shown. Trim the end of the tape into a flag and break off 1 inch of the toothpick. Repeat with the remaining toothpicks and tape.

2. Cut each fruit strip into 5 triangles, as shown, then set aside. Insert a flag into the top of each gumdrop.

3. Working with one cupcake at a time, cover it with frosting, then arrange 5 candy wedges around the top, as shown. Top with a gumdrop flag in the center (use more frosting to adhere it if needed). Repeat with the remaining cupcakes and ingredients.

Makes 12

Ingredients

12 sour red fruit strips

12 green gumdrops

12 un-frosted vanilla cupcakes

1 cup white frosting

Special Equipment

Washi tape

12 toothpicks

Tip

For instructions on how to create the toothpick flags, turn to page 135.

Sugar Rush Popcorn-Gumdrop Garland

Ingredients

1 package of popcorn, popped and cooled

2 (16-oz) bags of multicolored gumdrops

Tray of Never Land Star Marshmallows (page 99) or regular marshmallows

Tip

Make sure to use cooled, or even day-old, popcorn—it's easier to string!

In *Sugar Rush*, even the Christmas decorations are made out of candy, and with **Ralph** around to help, reaching the top branches of the Christmas tree is no trouble at all. Create a seasonal garland in the real world that is just as good to nibble on as it is to deck your halls with.

Directions

1. Have an adult help you thread a blunt sewing needle with fishing line, thread, or even unflavored waxed dental floss. Leave the tail end attached to the spool.

2. Choose a pattern of popcorn, gumdrops, and marshmallows to repeat. Begin stringing the pieces by piercing the needle through the center of each object and pushing the object down along the string.

3. Once your garland is long enough, have an adult help you cut the thread from the spool and tie knots at both ends to secure.

Little Green Gingerbread Alien Cookies

These lime green, candy-topped gingerbread cookies would make an *ooooh*-inspiring addition to any holiday cookie tray.

Directions

To Make the Dough

1. Ask an adult for help with the oven. Heat the oven to 375°F. Line two baking sheets with parchment paper. In a medium bowl, whisk together the flour, ginger, cinnamon, cloves, baking soda, and salt.

2. In a stand mixer fitted with the paddle attachment and set on medium-high speed, cream the butter and sugar until light and fluffy, about 3 minutes. Blend in the egg, followed by the molasses. Reduce the mixer's speed to low and blend in the flour mixture, one-third at a time.

3. Knead the dough a few times on a lightly floured surface. Halve it, then roll and flatten each portion into a disk. Wrap each in plastic and refrigerate 1 hour.

4. On a lightly floured surface, roll out one portion of the dough to ¼-inch thickness. Use a 3-inch oval cookie cutter to cut the dough. Arrange the cutouts on the baking sheets 2 inches apart. Gather and reroll the dough as needed.

5. Bake the cookies until slightly crisp around the edges and fully set, about 10 minutes, rotating the tray halfway through. Let them cool on the baking sheets 5 minutes, then transfer to a rack to cool completely.

To Make the Icing

1. Combine the sugar, meringue powder, and corn syrup with 6 tablespoons warm water in the bowl of a stand mixer fitted with a whisk attachment. Beat at medium speed until thickened but not stiff, adding food coloring as desired. If the icing is too thick, add another tablespoon water; if too thin, add another tablespoon sugar.

To Decorate the Cookies

1. Cover a cookie with icing, then press on three candy eyes, two gumdrop ears, and a fruit-candy antenna. Repeat with each cookie, and let the icing set. Use a food writer to add a mouth to each.

Ingredients

Dough

2 cups flour, plus more for dusting

1 tsp ground ginger

½ tsp ground cinnamon

¼ tsp ground cloves

½ tsp baking soda

¼ tsp kosher salt

½ cup (1 stick) unsalted butter, room temperature

½ cup dark brown sugar

1 egg, room temperature

¼ cup molasses

Icing

2 cups confectioners' sugar, plus extra as needed

1½ tsp meringue powder

1 Tbsp corn syrup

Green food coloring

Decorations

Candy eyes

Green gumdrops, halved from top to bottom

Green fruit-flavored candies, halved lengthwise

Black food writer

*Makes about 1 dozen
3- to 4-inch cookies*

Ingredients

2½ cups flour, plus more
for dusting

1 tsp baking powder

¼ tsp kosher salt

1 cup sugar

¾ cup (1½ sticks)
unsalted butter, softened

2 eggs,
room temperature

½ tsp vanilla extract

8 fruit-flavored hard
candies, lightly crushed

1 batch icing
(see page 117), optional

Tip

*For instructions on how to
cut and fill the center of each
cookie, turn to page 136.*

Glass Ornament Cookies

Leave Santa a plate of these special sugar cookies—the shiny and colorful centers resemble Cinderella's iconic glass slippers! You'll need a bit of patience to make them, but they're the perfect fit for any Christmas celebration.

Directions

1. In a small bowl, whisk together the flour, baking powder, and salt. In the bowl of a stand mixer fit with a paddle attachment and set on medium-high speed, beat the sugar and butter until light and fluffy, about 3 minutes. Add the eggs and vanilla and beat to incorporate. Reduce the mixer's speed to low and blend in the flour mixture one-third at a time. Do not overmix.

2. Turn the dough out onto a lightly floured surface and knead a few times. Roll it into a ball and flatten it into a disk. Cover with plastic, and refrigerate 30 minutes.

3. Ask an adult for help with the oven. Heat the oven to 350°F. Line two baking sheets with parchment paper. Roll out the dough to ¼-inch thickness. Cut out shapes with cookie cutters, and arrange the cookies on the baking sheets, spacing them 2 inches apart. Gather and reroll the dough as needed. Use smaller cutters to remove the center from each cookie, then freeze the cookies for 15 minutes.

4. Bake the cookies until set and slightly crisp, turning them once halfway through, about 12 minutes. Let the cookies cool on the pans for 5 minutes, then transfer them to a rack to cool completely. Reduce the oven temperature to 275°F.

5. Fill the center of each cookie with a few pieces of the crushed candy. Return to the oven and bake until the candies are melted, about 5 minutes. Let cool completely.

6. If desired, fill a piping bag or cookie decorator with icing and decorate each cookie before serving.

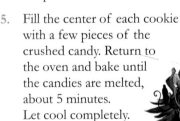

Mini Christmas Cannoli

Luca and Alberto love learning about human culture, such as a classic Italian dessert called cannoli, from their friend Giulia and her father. Adorn the ends of your cannoli with red and green sprinkles instead of chocolate chips for a special festive touch during the Christmas season.

Directions

1. In a medium bowl, whisk the ricotta until smooth. In another bowl, whip the heavy cream and confectioners' sugar until stiff peaks form, then gently fold in the ricotta, vanilla, lemon zest, and a pinch of cinnamon until combined. Transfer the mixture to the refrigerator and chill 1 hour, then transfer to a piping bag or plastic bag and snip the end.

2. Place the sprinkles in a small bowl. Use the piping bag to fill each cannoli shell, then dip both ends of each into the sprinkles. Refrigerate the cannoli until ready to serve.

Makes 1 dozen

Ingredients

¾ cup ricotta cheese, drained 1 hour

¼ cup heavy cream

2 Tbsp confectioners' sugar

½ tsp vanilla extract

½ tsp lemon zest

Pinch of ground cinnamon

12 mini cannoli shells

3 Tbsp Christmas sprinkles

Tip

To drain the ricotta, place it in a mesh strainer or doubled sheet of cheesecloth and let sit.

Makes 6

Ingredients

2 strips green sour tape candy

9 mini Swiss rolls

⅔ cup chocolate frosting

Red pearl sprinkles

Confectioners' sugar, for dusting

Tip

For easier frosting, remove the chocolate coating on each roll before covering with fresh frosting.

Mini Buche de Noel

In Parisian bakeries, like the ones the Aristocats love to stroll by in their neighborhood, you're bound to see traditional treats such as these tiny chocolate cakes decorated to resemble little tree trunks.

Directions

1. Trim the sour tape into 12 leaves. Set aside. Trim the ends of each Swiss roll so you can see its layers, and halve three of the rolls. Line a baking sheet with parchment paper.

2. Use a dot of chocolate frosting to attach a half roll to the side of a whole roll. With a small offset spatula or spoon, cover the cake with chocolate frosting. Add a few pearl sprinkle berries and two sour tape leaves. Repeat with the remaining ingredients. Lightly dust the cakes with confectioners' sugar before serving.

Baymax S'mores Brownie Bites

S'mores aren't just for sharing around a campfire—their toasty flavors also make this gooey chocolate brownie the perfect treat after a day of playing in the snow. Baymax's billowy snowman-like face forms a festive marshmallow topping to capture the winter fun.

Directions

1. Ask an adult for help with the oven. Heat the oven to 350°F and coat a mini muffin tin with cooking spray. Prepare the brownie batter according to the package directions, then fold in the graham cracker pieces.

2. Evenly divide the batter among the muffin tin wells and bake 10 minutes. Let cool slightly, then transfer to a rack to cool completely.

3. With an adult's help, melt the chocolate chips according to the package directions. Spoon a small amount onto the center of each brownie bite and attach a marshmallow to each, cut side down. Use a toothpick and the remaining melted chocolate to draw Baymax's face on each marshmallow. Let the chocolate set before serving.

Makes 2 dozen

Ingredients

Cooking spray

1 box chocolate chunk brownie mix

3 graham crackers, broken into small pieces

½ cup chocolate chips

12 large marshmallows, halved

Tip

If you don't have a mini muffin tin, you can also bake the brownies in a square dish and cut them into 16 mini squares before decorating. You'll need only 8 marshmallows.

Makes about 2 dozen

Ingredients

2 egg whites

¼ tsp cream of tartar

⅔ cup sugar, divided

Red and blue food coloring

⅓ cup white candy melts

Nonpareil sprinkles

Tip

If you'd like to make meringues in multiple colors, divide the meringue into portions and then add a different color to each.

You'll need a separate piping bag for each color.

Wonderland Meringues

When the snow keeps her inside, Alice daydreams about joining her friends in Wonderland for a whimsical Christmas tea. These dainty mushroom-shaped meringues are inspired by the delightful blooms that Alice encounters in the Tulgey Wood.

Directions

1. Ask an adult for help with the oven. Heat the oven to 300°F and line a baking sheet with parchment paper.

2. With a stand or handheld mixer set at medium speed, whisk the egg whites until frothy, about 1 minute. With the mixer still running, add the cream of tartar and 1 tablespoon of the sugar and blend well. Continue whisking the eggs and adding sugar, 1 tablespoon at a time and blending in thoroughly between each addition, until stiff peaks form, about 8 minutes more. Blend in the food coloring as directed on the package to make purple.

3. Place the meringue in a piping bag fitted with a large round tip (you'll need separate bags if using more than one color). On the baking sheet, pipe the meringue into 24 one-inch-wide stems, then 24 round dollops, spacing them 2 inches apart. Top the meringues with nonpareil sprinkles and place the pan in the oven, then bake 2 hours. Turn the oven off and let the meringues cool undisturbed, about 2 hours more.

4. Use a skewer to make a ½-inch-wide hole on the flat end (the underside) of each meringue mushroom cap. Carefully melt the candy according to the package directions. Dip the end of a meringue stem into the candy, then attach it to a meringue cap by inserting it onto the hole. Repeat with the remaining meringues and candy. Let the candy set, then store meringues in an airtight container until ready to serve.

Step-by-Step Instructions

Turn the page for step-by-step photos for some of the recipes—and you'll be a pro at creating dishes that are both delicious and eye-catching in no time.

Pooh Bear's Mini Honey Buns

Follow these steps to shape the buns into spirals.

1. Remove the biscuits from the tube.

2. Roll one biscuit portion of the dough into an 8- to 12-inch rope.

3. Wind the rope into a spiral.

4. Pinch the end to attach it to the dough spiral before placing it in the prepared muffin tin.

See the full recipe on page 24!

Ariel's Puff Pastry Stars

Learn to cut and fill these fruity pastries by following the steps below.

1. Use a paring knife to score the stars from corner to corner at the base of each point, being careful not to cut all the way through the dough.

2. After scoring, the stars should look like the photo above.

3. Add a dollop of cream cheese filling to the center of each star inside the score lines.

4. Top each star with sliced berries.

See the full recipe on page 26!

Lunar New Year Dumplings

Fill and fold your dumplings with this step-by-step guide.

1. Use your finger to wet the edges of a dumpling wrapper with water.

2. Add the filling to the center of the dumpling.

3. Fold the wrapper in half and pinch it closed in the center.

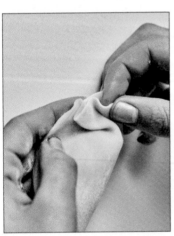 

4. Use your fingers to make two crimps on one end of the dumpling, as shown, then repeat with the opposite end.

See the full recipe on page 42!

Christmas Ribbon Salad

Prep like a chef with this guide to creating cucumber ribbons.

1. Gather your supplies: a knife, a peeler, and a cucumber.

2. Use the knife to trim the ends of the cucumber.

3. Lay the cucumber flat on your work surface and anchor it with one hand. Use your other hand to cut the cucumber into thin strips with a Y-shaped peeler, pulling the peeler toward you. Be careful to keep your fingers out of the way.

See the full recipe on page 80!

Hoppy Holidays Garden Veggie Wreath

Follow this guide to create the perfect berry shapes for your edible wreaths with a straw.

1. Trim the stem end of the pepper, halve it, and remove the seeds.

2. Press the end of a plastic straw into a pepper half, as shown.

3. Remove the cut pepper piece by pinching the end of the straw.

See the full recipe on page 94!

Dumbo's Big Top Candy Cane Cupcakes

Create your own mini circus flag using this step-by-step guide.

1. Gather your supplies: scissors, toothpicks, and washi tape.

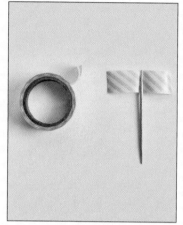

2. Attach a toothpick to the center of a 2-inch strip of washi tape.

3. Fold the pick into the tape keeping the edges of the tape aligned.

4. Trim a small triangle from the edge of the flag, as shown.

5. The flag should look like the photo above.

See the full recipe on page 112!

135

Glass Ornament Cookies

Use the guide below to fill your cookies with colorful crushed candy.

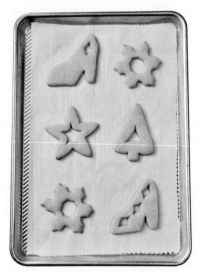

1. Arrange the cookies on a parchment-lined baking sheet, spacing them 2 inches apart.

2. Generously fill the center of each cookie with crushed candies, taking care to fill each to the top of the opening and as close to the edges as possible, as shown.

See the full recipe on page 118!

Dietary Considerations

Food allergies or preferences? No problem! Use this guide to check which recipes accommodate dairy-free, gluten-free, nut-free, vegan, and vegetarian diets—and which can be adapted to let everyone enjoy the meal. Recipes not included below may not be suitable for special diets. If using store-bought ingredients, always check the label or packaging to make sure they meet your dietary needs.

DF = dairy-free
GF = gluten-free
NF = nut-free
V = vegan
VEG = vegetarian

Breakfast

Rolly's Spotted Cranberry Pancakes   VEG
Monster-O's Spiced Breakfast Bars   VEG
Sleepy's Early-Riser Egg Biscuits   NF / VEG (if the bacon is left out or a vegetarian-friendly substitute is used)
Belle's Classic Winter Porridge   GF / VEG
Pooh Bear's Mini Honey Buns   NF / VEG
Ariel's Puff Pastry Stars   NF / VEG
Purr-fect French Toast   NF / VEG
New York City Breakfast Pizzettes   NF

Lunch

Sweet Dough Turnovers   NF / VEG (if the optional meat fillings are left out)
Arepas de Queso   GF / NF / VEG
Rapunzel's Pumpkin Hazelnut Soup   VEG (if cooked with vegetable stock)
Joyful Mac & Cheese   NF / VEG
Lunar New Year Dumplings   DF / NF
Festive Green Bean Casserole   NF / VEG
Rapunzel Pizza Braid   NF
Ham Musubi   DF / NF

Dinner

Lady and the Tramp Sheet Pan Meatballs and Sauce   NF
Aristocat-ic Quiche Marie   NF
Lightning McQueen's Pot Pie   NF
Woody's Cowboy Chili   DF / GF / NF
To Infinity and Beyond Meat Loaf   DF / NF
Sheet Pan Ratatouille with Smoked Sausage   DF / NF
Merida's Day-After-Christmas Sliders   NF

Dinner (*continued*)

Pinocchio's Pepperoni Pasta DF (if Parmesan cheese is left out) / NF
Pork Tenderloin Planks with Green Herb Sauce DF / GF / NF
Magic Hammer Chicken NF

Sides

Wreck-It Ralph's Smashed Potatoes DF / GF / NF / V / VEG
Snow White's Cinnamon Apples GF / NF / VEG
Chicken Long Rice DF / GF / NF
Christmas Ribbon Salad DF / GF / NF / V / VEG
Dreamy Winter Slaw GF / VEG

Snacks

Frozen Banana Dalmatian Pops GF / NF / VEG / DF and V
    (if dairy-free chocolate chips are used)
Ariel's Starfish Dip GF / NF / VEG
Aurora's Yummy Yogurt Dip GF / NF / VEG
Peanut Butter Puppy Chow VEG / NF / VEG
Hoppy Holidays Garden Veggie Wreath NF / VEG

Beverages

Never Land Hot Chocolate with Star Marshmallows DF (if non-dairy milk is used) / GF
Jiminy Cricket Milkshake NF / VEG
Aunt Cass's Apple Cider DF / GF / NF / V / VEG
Stitch's Hawaiian Eggnog GF / NF / VEG
Agua de Jamaica DF / GF / NF / V / VEG

Sweets

Sherwood Forest Peppermint Bark DF (if dairy-free white chocolate is used) / GF / NF
Dumbo's Big Top Candy Cane Cupcakes NF / VEG
Sugar Rush Popcorn-Gumdrop Garland DF / GF / NF
Little Green Gingerbread Alien Cookies NF / VEG
Glass Ornament Cookies NF / VEG
Mini Christmas Cannoli NF / VEG
Mini Buche de Noel NF / VEG
Baymax S'mores Brownie Bites NF
Wonderland Meringues DF / NF / VEG

Glossary

A

Allspice—a spice made from a type of berry

Apple cider vinegar—a type of vinegar made from apple juice

Arepas—flat, tortilla-like cakes originating in Latin America, made out of cornmeal and often stuffed with cheese or fillings

B

Bake—to cook ingredients in an oven using indirect heat around the food. Many ovens must first be set to a bake setting before the temperature is adjusted

Baking sheet—a flat metal pan used for baking, especially sweets like cookies, biscuits, or breads

Baste—to pour liquid over meat during cooking to keep it moist

Basting brush—a tool used to spread liquids evenly over the surfaces of food and cooking apparatuses

Bay leaf—the leaf of a bay tree, commonly used as an herb in Mediterranean cuisines

Beat—to quickly stir an ingredient or batter with a whisk, electric mixer, or spoon until it's smooth and/or fluffy

Blend—to combine two or more ingredients into a smooth mixture

Brioche—a rich, sweet French bread made with eggs and butter

Broil—to cook ingredients using direct heat over the food. Most ovens have broiling settings.

C

Candy melts—colored candy chips that are melted and used for baking and decorating

Cannoli—a classic Italian pastry typically consisting of fried dough wrapped in a tube shape around a sweet, creamy filling

Capers—the dried, pickled flower buds of the caper bush, common in Mediterranean cuisine

Cayenne pepper—a moderately spicy pepper used to flavor dishes

Challah—a braided bread of Ashkenazi Jewish origin that is made with eggs, flour, sugar, yeast, and water

Chives—a green, grasslike herb with a mild onion flavor. It's often used as a garnish.

Chop—to cut an ingredient into pieces that are roughly the same size

Cilantro—an herb also known as coriander, often used in Mexican cuisine

Cloves (garlic)—each segment of a garlic plant bulb

Cloves (spice)—a spice made from the dried flower buds of a tropical tree

Coconut oil—a type of oil made from coconut meat

Confectioners' sugar—a finely ground form of sugar, also known as powdered sugar

Cream—to blend ingredients, typically butter and sugar, into a soft and creamy mixture

Cream of coconut—a syrup made by sweetening coconut cream

Cream of tartar—a plant-based dry powder often used in baking

Crumbled—broken or rubbed into small pieces

D

Dice—to cut foods into small cubes (typically ¼-inch wide)

Dijon mustard—a smooth type of mustard made with white wine or wine vinegar, originating in Dijon, France

Dill—a sweet, delicate, green herb harvested from the flowering tops of dill plants

Drizzle—to slowly pour a thin stream of liquid or a melted ingredient over another food

Dumpling—portions of dough, typically wrapped around a filling like meat or vegetables

Dust—to lightly sprinkle a powdery ingredient, such as confectioners' sugar or flour. Rolling pins are often dusted with flour to keep them from sticking to piecrust, cookie dough, or other foods that are rolled out.

E

Extract—a concentrated flavoring made by soaking certain foods, such as vanilla beans, in water and/or other liquids

F

Feta—a crumbly, white cheese of Greek origin most often made of sheep or goat's milk

Fold—to gently blend ingredients by using a spatula to cut through the center of the mixture and then flip one half over the other. Stiff beaten egg whites are often folded, rather than stirred, into cake and soufflé recipes to keep as much air in the batter as possible.

G

Garnish—to decorate a prepared recipe with an herb, fruit, or other edible ingredient that adds color and/or texture

Gelatin—an animal-based protein used to stabilize and thicken foods such as jams, jellies, and marshmallows

Ginger—a root commonly used as a spice

Grate—to shred foods, such as coconut, carrots, cheese, or chocolate, into bits or flakes by rubbing them against a grater

Greek yogurt—a thick type of yogurt that has been strained

Ground—when a dry ingredient has been crushed into very small pieces, often with a powderlike texture

H

Herbes de Provence—a blend of dried herbs that is commonly used in French and Mediterranean cooking

Hibiscus flower—a tart, floral ingredient made from a hibiscus plant

J

Jarlsberg cheese—a type of mild cheese originating in Norway

K

Kitchen shears—scissors made specifically for cutting food

Knead—to repeatedly fold and press together dough until it is smooth and stretchy. Kneading traps air bubbles produced by the yeast, which is what makes the dough rise.

L

Long rice—A traditional Hawaiian dish, usually made with mung bean noodles rather than rice

M

Marinate—to soak food in a flavored liquid for an extended period of time so that the food absorbs the flavor before cooking. The flavored liquid is called a marinade.

Masarepa flour—a precooked, ground corn flour commonly used in Latin American dishes

Meringue—a type of dessert traditionally made with whipped egg whites and sugar

Meringue powder—an egg white substitute used to make meringue, icing, and other baked goods

Mince—to chop ingredients, such as garlic cloves, gingerroot, or fresh herbs, extra fine. This evenly distributes the flavor in the dish you are cooking.

Molasses—a thick syrup made from sugarcane, used as a sweetener

Mung bean noodles—also known as glass noodles, these transparent noodles are made from mung bean starch and are commonly used in Asian cuisines

Musubi—a traditional Hawaiian dish inspired by Japanese cuisine, made with canned ham, rice, and nori

N

Nonpareils sprinkles—tiny, round sprinkles used for decorating baked goods

Nori—thin sheets of dried, mildly sweet seaweed, mainly used in Japanese cuisine as a food wrap for sushi

Nutmeg—a spice made from the seed of a tropical tree

O

Offset spatula—a decorating tool with a thin, flat blade and rounded tip, used for spreading frosting or batter

Oregano—an herb commonly used in Mediterranean cuisines

P

Panko bread crumbs—a flaky type of bread crumb originating in Japan, made from baked, crustless bread and typically used to coat other food

Paprika—a spice made from ground dried bell or chili peppers

Parchment paper—heat-resistant paper used to line a baking sheet so cookies and other foods won't stick to the pan when you bake them

Paring knife—a small utensil used to delicately peel or cut fruits and vegetables

Persian cucumbers—a type of mini cucumber that is narrow and seedless

Pinch—a small amount of a dry ingredient, such as salt or a ground spice, added to a recipe with your fingertips

Piping bag—a cone-shaped bag with a pointed end used to dispense batter, frosting, or other soft-food mixtures. To use one, snip the pointed end of the bag and fit a piping tip inside. Fill the bag with your chosen frosting or topping, then twist the open end to seal the bag. Pipe the mixture by pushing it from the sealed end.

Pizzette—a small pizza

Produce—fresh fruits and/or vegetables

Puff pastry—a light, flaky pastry made by combining thin layers of butter and dough

Puree—to blend food until it is completely smooth

Q

Quiche—a traditionally French tart made with pastry crust, egg custard, and savory fillings

R

Ratatouille—a vegetable-based dish that originated in the Provence region of France

Ricotta—a creamy type of cheese, originating in Italy, made from liquid leftover during the production of other cheeses

Rosemary—an herb commonly used in Mediterranean cuisines

S

Saucepan—a high-sided pan, usually with handles meant for cooking foods on a stovetop

Scallion—a long, green onion with a small bulb on its end

Separate egg whites—to divide egg whites (the clear portion of the egg) from their yolks (the yellow portion). To do it, crack the egg and pour its contents into one of the shell halves. Working over a bowl, tip the yolk back and forth into each shell half, letting the white fall into the bowl. Slide the yolk into a separate bowl.

Sesame oil—an oil created from seeds of the sesame plant

Sesame seeds—the seeds of the sesame plant, commonly used as a seasoning

Shallot—a purple-skinned, bulb-shaped onion with a mild flavor

Shred—to pull or cut an ingredient into many thin strips

Simmer—to cook food on the stovetop in liquid heated just to the point at which small bubbles rise to the surface

Skillet—a flat-bottomed, shallow pan with a long handle used for cooking on a stovetop

Snip—to use kitchen scissors to cut an ingredient into small pieces

Soften—to warm an ingredient such as butter (either by setting it out at room temperature or heating it in a microwave) until it is easy to combine with a mixture

Star anise—a star-shaped, licorice-flavored fruit that is dried and used as a spice. It is used in many Asian cuisines.

Steep—to soak an ingredient in water or another liquid, to infuse the liquid with the ingredient's flavor

Strain—to remove liquid from an ingredient or mixture by pouring it into a colander, metal sieve, or cheesecloth.

The solids are trapped in the colander, sieve, or cloth and liquid drains away

Sushi rice—a sticky type of short-grain white rice originating in Japan and commonly used to make sushi

Swiss rolls—a type of sponge cake filled with flavored cream, rolled into the shape of a log

T

Thyme—an herb commonly used in Mediterranean cuisines

To taste—just enough of a certain ingredient, typically one or more spices, to improve the flavor of a dish

Toss—to mix solid ingredients by gently combining them

W

Washi tape—a decorative crafting tape

Whip—to beat air into an ingredient, such as cream or egg whites, until it is light and fluffy

Whisk—a long-handled kitchen utensil with a series of wire or plastic loops at the end used to rapidly beat eggs, cream, or other liquids. *Whisk* is also a verb that means "to use a whisk."

White pepper—a spice made from the dried fruit of the pepper plant. It is more mild than black pepper.

Worcestershire sauce—a liquid condiment typically made with a vinegar base that can add a tangy flavor to dishes

Z

Zest—a flavorful ingredient created from the outermost rind (or peel) of citrus fruits like lemons, limes, and oranges. To zest a citrus fruit, ask an adult for help to find the right kitchen tool, like a zester or rasp grater. Hold the fruit over a bowl and use the zester or grater to gently scrape the outer peel, stopping when you reach the white part of the peel.

Index

Page numbers in *italics* are pictures.